T0207701

# TURNING POINTS:
## CHARACTER FORGED IN THE
## "CRUCIBLE OF COMBAT"

Carolyn Salerno-Brydges, EdD

Order this book online at www.trafford.com
or email orders@trafford.com

Most Trafford titles are also available at major online book retailers.

Editor: Jon M. Corey, PhD.

Print information available on the last page.

ISBN: 978-1-6987-0904-8 (sc)
ISBN: 978-1-6987-0905-5 (hc)
ISBN: 978-1-6987-0906-2 (e)

Library of Congress Control Number: 2021916221

*Trafford rev. 10/12/2021*

www.trafford.com
North America & international
toll-free: 844-688-6899 (USA & Canada)
fax: 812 355 4082

# DEDICATION

In memoriam I want to dedicate this book of heroes' stories to my late husband, Commander Richard R. Brydges. What I thought would be a forthright effort is now far more difficult than I could have ever envisioned, as I attempted to summarize in this short space what a genuinely wonderful husband, father, friend, gentleman, and Navy officer Rick was—despite his facing a series of long-term challenges most individuals could not endure.

Rick encompassed every quality and trait that makes for a truly "good man." He was intelligent, compassionate, loving, and dedicated by any measure. Moreover, Rick was the love of my life—and he will be always. He was a cherished comrade, and he was respected by everyone with whom he came in contact. Comparisons to Rick R. Brydges simply cannot be made as he stood out as a steadfast role model for others.

He was truly a "...*Sequoia among the pines....*"

*His Loving Wife, Carolyn Brydges*

# CONTENTS

# FOREWORD

MAJ Jon M. Corey, PhD

No one can speak about the souls of the men who served in the Vietnam War except those service members who actually fought on the ground, in the air, and on the sea. Only these special individuals can describe their combat experiences, affording us powerful insights into their personalities, behaviors, and morals with vivid descriptions of life-altering warfare events that remolded each man in his own "crucible of combat." Life-altering decisions and close combat actions have awe-inspiring and permanent impacts on individuals and recast the very core of every combatant, as well as their values, convictions, vulnerabilities, strengths, and perceptions. The accounts of closely contested battle situations and ultimate survival are exclusive life scenarios full of unexpected plot twists, with capture, injury or death possible consequences.

As I noted based on my experience as a professor of psychology and my citations for the Silver Star, Distinguished Flying Cross, Bronze Star for Valor, Air Medal for Valor, Combat Infantryman Badge, and Purple Heart, military soldiers fight with great honor, unbounded tenacity, and limitless courage primarily to defend their fellow troops—nothing is more important. Taking risks for one's military unit and comrades and surviving are uniquely powerful, and doing so internalizes one's thinking and loyalty on a virtually permanent basis.

In studying the accounts of harrowing battle situations and ultimate survival on the ground, in the air, and on the sea by military personnel who were undeniably transformed forever by combat, we can hope to understand how military leaders accomplish great things and appreciate what drives them and their fellow service members.

The American War Library estimates that approximately 610,000 Americans who served on land, in the air, or in the waters of Vietnam between 1954 and 1975 are alive today. Many of the life-altering, combat-intense "turning points" shared by some of these armed services officers and enlisted personnel highlight these individuals' values in providing a lasting legacy for their families and nationwide patriotic organizations via a virtual "crucible of combat." These firsthand accounts memorialize ideals based on love, loyalty, duty, and acts of transformational leadership to deal with the challenges of life, as well as principles of working together as families and comrades.

# INTRODUCTION

MAJ Jon M. Corey, PhD

As no one without actual experience can speak about the souls of the men who served in the Vietnam War—except those service members who actually fought on the ground, in the air, and on the sea—only these special individuals can describe their battle experiences, affording us powerful insights into their personalities, behaviors, and morals—vivid descriptions of life-altering warfare events that remolded each man in his own "crucible of combat." Life-altering decisions and close combat actions have awe-inspiring and permanent impacts on those who served in direct battle, and more often than not, impromptu fighting scenarios inevitably reveal and recast the very core of all service members who faced an armed enemy or were cast into highly dangerous situations, as well as their previously unknown values, convictions, vulnerabilities, strengths, and perceptions. The accounts of dire close warfare situations and ultimate survival are exclusive life scenarios full of unexpected plot twists with capture or death possible, if not probable, consequences. Herein, we can summarily compare our experiences and knowledge of the personalities, behaviors, and morals of individuals during peacetime with those "chosen few" who were undeniably transformed forever by combat, and consequently, we can somewhat better understand how military leaders accomplish great things by having an inner knowledge of their men and what drives them.

According to the National Archives and Records Administration in 2008, there were 58,220 US military fatal casualties; a million Vietnamese were also killed. Although the United States was taking a military stand against communist aggression, the Vietnam War did not go down in history as a success—although the American military was never once defeated in any major battle during this entire time. The role of the United States in the Vietnam War escalated into a full commitment from 1955 to 1973. During these twenty long years, 9,087,000 military personnel served on active duty during the Vietnam era, and from 1964 to 1975, 2,709,918 Americans served in Vietnam. President Nixon ended all US military support and interventions in Vietnam and the rest of Southeast Asia in 1973. Ultimately, Vietnam fell completely to communism as the United States Congress failed to honor America's promise and commitments to maintain the military forces of South Vietnam.

# TURNING
# POINTS

# BAPTISM BY FIRE

CDR Richard Ross Brydges, PhD

My name is Richard Ross Brydges, retired US Navy commander. As I reflect on the military career that ultimately led me to serve as an attack pilot during the Vietnam War, I see the origins of that career in my early life. In high school, for example, I was acknowledged for my skills playing football as a quarterback and was elected captain of the football and basketball teams. Consequently, the Naval Academy Athletic Association offered me an appointment to Annapolis, where I engaged in intensive military training, and also continued to play football, though at the far more rigorous level of college athletics. After graduating from the academy as an ensign with the class of 1967, I volunteered for naval aviation.

The turning point that forged my character in combat and afterward took place after approximately eighteen months of my flight training to become a navy attack pilot, flying an A-7 Corsair II, a subsonic light attack aircraft. My combat story began with my deployment, and by being designated "all up round," which is a Navy term for a fully operational person fit for duty as a naval aviator with Attack Squadron 82. This priority distinction entitled me to the "rite of passage" to receive special treatment to join the squadron that was already deployed to Southeast Asia in the Gulf of Tonkin, off Vietnam.

In June 1970, I arrived at my aircraft carrier, the USS *Coral Sea*, which was deployed in the Gulf of Tonkin; the operations officer soon told me to "join up and shut up" to replace a lost pilot. My mission was to engage the enemy, which was flying their formidable MiG-17 and MiG-21 fighters, and to drop bombs on designated enemy positions. These advanced targets were assigned to me by warfare intelligence sources, and "targets of opportunity" were also directed to me by forward air controllers (FACs) flying low in single-engine planes about two thousand feet aboveground. As a flight lieutenant, my first daunting "reality check" was my landing on the USS *Coral Sea* during a pitch-black night while experiencing vertigo. I now term this phase of my professional and personal experience as "baptism by fire."

The cycle time for each flight was one hour and thirty minutes from takeoff time to landing back on the ship. Two flights were scheduled, each beginning between sunrise and sunset in the Gulf of Tonkin. Enemy targets included supplies, cargo, munitions, and weapons that were being transported under jungle cover via the Ho Chi Minh Trail and outlining pathways, a formidable network of roads built from North Vietnam to South Vietnam through the neighboring countries of Laos and Cambodia. I started a roll-in from ten thousand feet with my aircraft for my bombing run on a target designated by a FAC, and a flash before my eyes bore the reality that enemy ground-to-air missiles were shooting at me. I remember thinking, *What am I doing here?* I was flying as a wingman on a two-plane sortie, and my original mission was to follow directions from the FAC to a suspected target and to dodge upcoming 20mm antiaircraft flak fire. Encountering enemy fighter and ground-based fire certainly seemed a possibility—but not a probability at that time!

The outcome was that we executed our mission—dropped our 10,800-pound bombs over jungle vegetation from where the firing was coming, turned our planes, and went back out to sea to rendezvous with our carrier. I was told by the lead aircraft pilot that this maneuver was part of the "indoctrination" process!

I sustained no physical injuries in combat flight during that mission—only the awareness and appreciation of surviving after being attacked by enemy MiG-17s and MiG-21s, as well as by intense ground fire from 20*mm* ground-based air defense guns. I vividly recalled my flight training and experience, the preparations I had received for combat, burgeoning sense of survival, the overwhelming need to survive while taking off the ship's runway, and the stark realization that the enemy had been shooting at me—but I continued dropping my bombs, completing my mission, and landing safely back on the carrier. After landing on the ship at night and walking across the deck back to the ready room, I felt relieved I had survived the "crucible of combat" and remember thinking, *By the grace of God go I!* Subsequently, I was awarded an Air Medal for this act of aerial achievement. Ultimately, I completed sixty assigned missions flying my A-7 Corsair II during my tour of duty.

The memory of my role in these missions created a lasting bond with my squadron mates that has endured across five decades now. The turning points and lessons learned in the "crucible of combat" during my Vietnam War experience—although at the time I had little context about the purpose of the missions and the operations that were executed over Vietnam—are that my determination to accomplish my missions required practice, strategy, and reliance on my critical support teams in the air and on the ship. These combat lessons learned during those times have endured and have continued to influence my life with my family, friends, and colleagues. I retired after twenty-five years of active duty from the Navy with Sea Service Deployment Ribbon, Vietnam Service Medal, National Defense Service Medal, Navy Air Medals for Valor with Six Strike/

Flight Designations, Navy Commendation Medal, Meritorious Unit Commendation Medal, Navy Battle "E" Ribbon, and Vietnam Service Medal/with Bronze Star.

My "crucible of combat" experience continues today with my Parkinson's disease. The US Department of Veterans Affairs has acknowledged "Agent Orange," the name given to an herbicide used by the US military as a means of warfare during the Vietnam War as a cause of Parkinson's disease for 150,000 veterans who served during the Vietnam War. As a result of my combat in Vietnam, I contracted not only Parkinson's disease but also cancer. I continue to live each day with relative relief by reminiscing about landing safely on the carrier at night after daily combat, with continued determination to accomplish my daily mission. Each day, I continue to practice strategies for health and to rely on my critical support team—including my family and, of course, the many memories of my navy team members as they were in the air and on the ship. With life challenges resulting from Vietnam combat, as in all sports, there are winners and losers. Winners require a heart for the game, determination, practice, strategy—with team members supporting one another. The key challenge for people with Parkinson's disease is when and if they decide they are going to be winners or losers. If one is going to be a winner, one has to create a network with discipline and heart, a support team that can help one move from an individual journey to a collective one. Like combat, life is most successful when it is a collective experience.

I have given presentations on my career topics: (a) graduating from Annapolis, (b) flying with the navy in Vietnam, (c) doing strategic planning at the Pentagon, (d) teaching calculated development for businesses in the private sector, (e) earning a doctoral degree in leadership from the University of San Diego, (f) living with Parkinson's disease, and (g) knowing the joys of life as the grace of God goes with me. With so much happiness and appreciation for my life, knowing I have so little of my own left, my story is my attempt to encourage everyone to do their best with limited resources and despite great challenges. I encourage everybody to visualize goals to invite and nurture the extraordinary powers of the individual; have the courage to live and play the game of life with heart, confidence, determination, and passion; and cherish the belief in a win–win scenario as they also embrace the grace of God.

John Adams said this so eloquently on Independence Day in 1776:

*I am well aware of the toil and blood and treasure it will cost us to maintain this declaration, and support and defend these states. Yet through all the gloom, I see the rays of ravishing light and glory. I can see that the end is worth all the means. This is our day of deliverance.*

And as Rear Admiral David Glasgow Farragut commanded during the Battle of Mobile Bay in 1864, he said:

*Damn the torpedoes, full speed ahead!*

Such quotes embody my personal experience in the "crucible of combat" in Vietnam and my experience at present as a survivor of Parkinson's and cancer. I too can "see that the end is worth all the means," and I am committed to moving forward with my team "full speed ahead!"

# DIFFERENT SITUATIONS–BUT THE SAME DYNAMICS!

MAJ Jon M. Corey, PhD

My having written the introduction to this book, as well as my prior contribution of an individualized chapter more than a decade earlier to a previous similar effort based on my award of the Bronze Star for Valor in *Leadership Moments: Turning Points That Changed Lives and Organizations* in authoring some key "lessons learned" I had garnered as a result of my combat experience in Vietnam, I thought I had exhausted all experiential, rational, and pragmatic "after action" insights that I could share in this newer publication. There simply was not much more knowledge I could add to this up-to-date iteration to highlight or to reaffirm what had already been published regarding how combat changes individuals, the way they subsequently live their lives, and the evolution of their follow-on behaviors, moral codes, and principles. All combatants, it seemed, developed and embraced a novel set of postcombat attitudes and perspectives unique to themselves— there was no pro forma template to which everyone adhered although there was, paradoxically, a continuum of generalizations regarding warfare that could be identified by military personnel dramatically involved in it.

Moreover, upon reflecting and progressively becoming more knowledgeable of my and others' combat actions and several evolving philosophies over many years, I determined there was still more understanding to be extrapolated and gleaned based on the Vietnam combat tour I had, all inclusive of the insights of comrades who had likewise endured and survived—and those individuals who were uniquely privy to the crucible of combat. I needed to ferret these phenomena out with a deeper, perhaps an even more insightful effort—employing more of a psychological bend based on my professional civilian experience and university education. As I purported in the introduction to this book, "life's takeaways" for those fortunate or unfortunate few as a result of intense combat can be positive—but negative as well—depending on one's or others' often unsung expectations, unacknowledged perceptions, or unrecognized principles.

As background, my temporary duty was as an army first lieutenant during May 1969 with a Fifth Special Forces (airborne) unit in Nha Trang, RVN. The RECONDO command trained elite long-range patrol members from many allied countries, and its tremendously rigorous and comprehensive clandestine battle course was noted as being *the deadliest school on earth* as its "graduation exercise" consisted of five-man squads going into largely uncontested, dangerous enemy areas with the prime purposes of securing information and eliminating soldiers of the North Vietnamese Army and the Vietcong; successful completion of the program earned every special recon soldier a unique permanent identification number. I was sent by my primary headquarters, the Twenty-Third Infantry Division (AMERICAL), to the Fifth Special Forces (airborne) unit in anticipation of being subsequently assigned to a SECRET ground mission on an isolated fire base along the Cambodian border, *"Operation Western Pistol,"* which involved Russians, Soviet helicopters, foreign mercenary pilots, and other unrevealed contingencies.

While on a RECONDO reconnaissance mission, our five-man long-range patrol encountered headlong a reinforced North

Vietnamese army company of approximately three hundred veteran troops in the Dong Bo Sacred Area, and an intense running firefight erupted that lasted approximately two hours. None of the troops in my patrol escaped being wounded, and as circumstances had it, on multiple occasions, I ended up charging enemy soldiers and machine gun emplacements using my automatic rifle and hand grenades, waving off an air evacuation to thwart a pending enemy ambush of the aircraft, dragging wounded troops to safety, destroying NVA soldiers "close up," causing secondary explosions in the enemy's area, and finally getting my patrol extracted from the area. Had we not been killed but captured, our lives would have been very limited, torturous, and worthless as the NVA/VC had bounties on everyone in our type of unit, especially those wearing Special Forces insignia or RANGER tabs. Although all five of us survived, a subsequent but rapid flyover recon revealed dozens of enemy dead. Details of this action are in the included official Silver Star citation.

In addition to what I noted in the earlier book I referenced, based on my award of the Bronze Star for Valor, as well as the Silver Star noted above, follow-on citations for the Distinguished Flying Cross, Air Medal for Valor, and Combat Infantryman Badge, plus discussions with others involved in close combat situations—a virtual continuum—I determined that although all such combatants own their individualized experiences, coupled with both the constructive and undesirable consequences of them, there remained some precepts that are immutable across the board. I believe they include, but are not limited to, the following wide range of dynamics, and if they do not fully qualify for or constitute what would be termed "lessons learned," they remain worthy of acknowledgment, acceptance, and awareness in furthering our understanding of war and its impacts on combatants.

***There exists an almost magnetic allure of war for many individuals.*** Many military personnel relish being in situations where they are challenged and fearful but supremely confident of the outcomes, primarily based on their bonding with their compatriots. This is the ethos of the "warrior" mentality, irrespective of which military branch they serve.

*Soldiers will fight with great honor, unbounded tenacity, and limitless courage primarily to defend their fellow troops.* They afford priority of their lives to their "comrades in arms" over all other considerations such as patriotism, fear of the enemy, political ideologies, "mom and apple pie," and other similar drivers. Their personal safety is secondary to that of their unit members, only followed by their drive to complete their missions. All considerations of personal or organizational failure, despite the potential dire consequences of their tactical situations, are often and best characterized as "emotion superseding logic" in assessing their actions when one reads the stories of their heroism and self-sacrifices. History is rife with documented accounts of camaraderie being the mainstay of crucial enemy encounters and pitched battles characterized by individual loyalty and the "intimacy of close combat" within the "brotherhood" of military endeavors.

*A sense of belonging is most powerful.* Taking great risks for one's military unit—and surviving—is uniquely powerful, and even if traumatized, it internalizes one's thinking, loyalty, and identification on a virtually permanent basis. Consider how many nonmilitary-related individuals will work for major business organizations for even a few years and, afterward, for several decades to come—if not the rest of their lives—still identify with those business organizations? There are few, if any. The armed services stand alone in garnering virtual lifelong affiliations and allegiances, largely irrespective of the length or contributions of one's military service.

*Enjoying the "sting of battle" is not irrational.* Many combatants miss situations where there are great challenges against other forces, which are incredibly demanding and intense endeavors; it is rooted in our DNA to take risks and often for men, especially, to not learn from dangerous or deadly encounters. Where would we be if early hunters were injured or their fellow tribesmen were killed hunting dangerous prey—and these early stalkers decided based on prior "lessons learned" they would not do so again the next day? Certainly, if such is not rooted in our DNA, the lust for challenge and danger while supporting one's comrades can be addictive.

*Sacrifice is paramount.* Examine most fraternity hazing practices, university entrance requirements, and rigorous organization or sports indoctrination rituals—and even their semi-lasting effects. Then they virtually "metastasize" these paradigms into the rigors of far more demanding military training, especially for elite combat units (e.g., Army RANGERS, Navy fighter pilots, Air Force Pararescue, Navy SEALs, Marine Corps Raiders, Coast Guard Deployable Specialized Forces, etc.)—and the élan they ultimately engender. Nothing else compares.

While focusing on the overall dynamics and consequences borne by any armed services member exposed to the crucible of close combat, it is just as important for other individuals to recognize in somewhat more detail the enduring and salient effects on each fighter that, as above, remain worthy of acknowledgement, acceptance, and awareness in furthering our understanding of war and its impacts on warriors:

*He is addicted to war.* War is horrible, but there is nothing like a "life-and-death" fight to make one feel truly alive. The adrenaline rush is tremendous, and it can never be replaced. Succeeding in combat defines a warrior, places him in a brotherhood where he is always welcome and understood. The civilian world has its adrenaline junkies as well; ask any retired firefighter, police officer, or emergency room staff if they miss it; however, those in such careers never fully experience the intensity, frequency, and duration that comes with actual combat.

*Living and moving forward in Life for these gallant individuals is manifestly harder.* It generally accepted that it is easier for a combat veteran to more readily die for his buddies as they become more bonded than do family members.

*"The training kicks in" means something very different to those involved in direct battle.* For example, it is essential warfare doctrine that when ambushed by a superior force, the correct response is ",,,Apply maximum firepower and break contact...." A warrior has to be able to respond to threat with minimal time pondering choices; there can be no focus groups or time-outs to seek opinions. While this is life-saving in combat, it is not helpful in the much slower-paced civilian world. A better rule in the civilian world would be to give a reaction proportionate to the provocation. "Small provocation, small response" (but this could get troops killed on the battlefield). When the training becomes second nature, a warrior might take any adrenaline rush as a cue to "apply maximum firepower." Period. This can become particularly unfortunate if someone or some experience starts to create a threat.

*He is often afraid to get attached to anyone because he has learned that the people he loves get killed, and he cannot face that pain again.* He may make an exception for his children, but that will be instinctual and he will probably not be able to explain his actions.

*He knows the military exists for a reason.* The sad fact is that a military exists ultimately to kill people and break things. This was true of our beloved "Greatest Generation" warriors of WWII, and it remains true to this day. Technically, a combat vet—a warrior—might well be a killer, as are his military friends. He may have a hard time seeing that this does not make him a murderer. Although they might look similar at first glance, he is a sheepdog protecting the herd, not a wolf trying to destroy it. The emotional side of killing in combat is complex. He may not know how to feel about what he's seen or done, and he may not expect his feelings to change over time. Warriors can experience moments of profound guilt, shame, and self-hatred. He may have experienced a momentary elation at "scoring one for the good guys," then been horrified that he celebrated killing a human being. He may view himself as a truly bad person for having those emotions, or for having gotten used to killing because it happened often—or even once.

*He's had to cultivate explosive anger in order to survive in combat.* He may have grown up with explosive anger (i.e., violent alcoholic father; threatening neighborhood; etc.) as well.

*He may have been only 19 when he first had to make a life and death decision for someone else.* What kind of skills does a 19-year-old have to deal with that kind of responsibility? One of combat veteran friend put it this way: "...You want to know what frightening is? It's a 19-year-old kid who's had a sip of that power over life and death that war gives him. It's a boy who, despite all the things he's been taught, knows that he likes it. It's a 19-year-old who's just lost a friend, and is angry, pumped-up, and scared, and determined that '...some bastard is gonna pay...!'"

*He may believe that he's the only one who feels this way; eventually he may realize that at least other combat vets understand.* On some level, he doesn't want you to understand, because that would mean you had shared his most horrible experience, and he wants someone to remain innocent. To place some relativity to the terrible experiences and exposures infantry ground soldiers faced in Viet Nam compared to America's prior wars and other major conflicts, it is fact that the typical U.S. Army infantryman in the South Pacific during World War II saw about 40 days of combat in FOUR years, approximately 10 days in an ENTIRE year. However, due to the increased mobility and logistical support made possible by the incorporation of transport and attack helicopters for the first time in combat, the typical U.S. Army infantryman in Vietnam saw about 240 days of combat in only ONE year! Moreover, a total of 58,148 U.S. troops were killed and 304,000 were wounded out of 2.7 million who served and the percentage of American service members who died is similar to other wars—but it is little known to the general public that despite vast increases due to the helicopters' mobility in enhancing the rapidity of battlefield medical evacuations—and the development of far greater field medical and hospital capabilities than those available during World War II—Viet Nam combat-related amputations or crippling wounds were 300% HIGHER than in World War II.

*He doesn't accept that you have a "mama bear" inside of you, that probably any of us could kill in defense of someone if we needed to.* Imagine your reaction if someone pointed a weapon at your child. Would it change your reaction if a child pointed a weapon at your son or daughter?

*When others don't understand, he needs them to give him the benefit of the doubt.* He wishes others also to realize that his issues really are not about others, although others may step in them sometimes. Truly, the last thing he wants is for others to become casualties of his war.

In sum, I do not have the eloquence to round out or to exemplify further what I have assumed to be "chapter and verse" in regard to any lessons learned or takeaways, so I embody my thoughts within Shakespeare's "Saint Crispin's Day Speech" wherein Henry V emotionally urged his men at Agincourt—who were isolated and vastly outnumbered by the French—to recall how the English had previously inflicted great defeats upon the French:

*"...We few, we happy few, we band of brothers;*
*For he to-day that sheds his blood with me*
*Shall be my brother; be he ne'er so vile,*
*This day shall gentle his condition.*
*And gentlemen in England now a-bed*
*Shall think themselves accurs'd they were not here,*
*And hold their manhoods cheap whiles any speaks*
*That fought with us upon Saint Crispin's day...."*

And because of Henry V's dynamic leadership, the English were again victorious!

EXAMPLES OF CLOSE COMBAT CITATIONS FOR
THE SILVER STAR AND DISTINGUISHED FLYING CROSS

Headquarters, Americal Division Artillery
APO San Francisco 96374

GENERAL ORDERS
NUMBER   1344

10 February 1970

AWARD OF THE SILVER STAR MEDAL

1. TC 439. The following AWARD is announced.

COREY, JON M. 183-36-0072, FIRST LIEUTENANT, AIR DEFENSE ARTILLERY
Battery G, 55th Artillery (RB), Americal Division Artillery APO 96374
Awarded: Silver Star Medal
Date of Service: 27 May 1969
Theater: Republic of Vietnam
Authority: By direction of the President under the provisions of the Act of
Congress approved 9 July 1918.
Reason: For extraordinary heroism while participating in ground operations against
a hostile force in the Republic of Vietnam. First Lieutenant Corey dis-
tinguished himself by exceptionally valorous actions on 27 May 1969 while
serving as a Long Range Patrol Leader with the 5th Special Forces Group
(ABN) MACV Recondo School. Lieutenant Corey's five man team was enroute
to a landing zone extraction point in the Dong Bo area when it made contact with the point element of an estimated reinforced North Vietnamese
Army company. An immediate, intense fire fight erupted and the patrol's
point man was seriously wounded. Lieutenant Corey, using rapid and exceptionally sound judgment, deployed his man in the best positions the
lightly forested area could offer. Lieutenant Corey, realizing that the
only way to rescue the wounded man was to silence an enemy machine gun
and automatic weapons position, managed to crawl to a location close
enough to destroy the element with two hand grenades, although he was
under intense enemy fire. Lieutenant Corey then charged two other enemy
soldiers, destroying them with rifle fire and dispersing several others.
Lieutenant Corey then dragged the wounded man approximately twenty yards
to a position of relative safety, where he then began to direct exceptionally
accurate and heavy support fire on the enemy unit from the gunship escort
helicopters which had previously been enroute to the landing zone. As
the evacuation helicopter approached, Lieutenant Corey noted a squad of
enemy soldiers attempting to organize an ambush for the aircraft, which
he waved off. Lieutenant Corey, then openly exposing himself to enemy
fire, moved to a position which afforded him an opportunity to direct
M-79 and rifle fire at the enemy position, which caused a secondary
explosion in the enemy area, thwarting the ambush and routing the North
Vietnamese element. The entire enemy unit withdrew and Lieutenant Corey
administered first aid to the wounded man and supervised the safe evacuation of his patrol. First Lieutenant Corey's personal heroism, professional
competence, and devotion to duty are in keeping with the highest traditions
of the military service, and reflect great credit upon himself, the
Americal Division, and the United States Army.

FOR THE COMMANDER:

OFFICIAL:

LARRY D. FLOWERS
1LT, AGC

T. H. TACKABERRY
Colonel, GS
Chief of Staff

DEPARTMENT OF THE ARMY
Headquarters, American Division
APO San Francisco 96374

GENERAL ORDERS
NUMBER 1343

9 February 1970

AWARD OF THE DISTINGUISHED FLYING CROSS

2.  TC 439.  The following AWARD is announced.

COREY, JON M., 183-36-0072, FIRST LIEUTENANT, AIR DEFENSE ARTILLERY,
Headquarters and Headquarters Battery, 1st Battalion, 82d Artillery, American
Division Artillery APO 96374
Awarded: Distinguished Flying Cross
Date of action: 9 September 1969
Theater:  Republic of Vietnam
Authority:  By direction of the President under the provisions of the Act of
        Congress, approved 2 July 1926.
Reason:  For heroism while participating in aerial flight as evidenced by
        voluntary action above and beyond the call of duty in the Republic
        of Vietnam:  LT Corey distinguished himself by exceptionally valorous
        actions on 9 September 1969 while serving as an aerial forward observer
        with the American Division Artillery while on a reconnaissance mission
        in the Tien Phuoc area.  After spotting enemy troop movements on the
        ground, LT Corey consistently called in and effectively directed air
        and artillery strikes on a North Vietnamese Army troop concentration
        in spite of exceptionally heavy enemy ground fire, which hit his air-
        craft in several places.  During the engagement LT Corey and his
        pilot located a 12.7mm dual heavy machine gun emplacement which had
        previously shot down one other U.S. aircraft and had caused damage
        to their own helicopter.  As friendly jet fighters had been unable
        to destroy the position, LT Corey and his pilot, who were both struck
        by shrapnel, elected to attack the enemy position in their LOH,
        utilizing white phosphorous grenades to destroy the machine gun
        emplacement as well as a confirmed squad size enemy unit.  While
        enroute to their base LZ, LT Corey demonstrated extensive experience
        and keen judgment as he greatly assisted the more seriously wounded
        aircraft commander in successfully crash landing their extensively
        damaged helicopter.  LT Corey's tenacious and aggressive actions
        were primarily responsible for the great success of the entire mission
        and the safe return of the aircraft.  LT Corey's outstanding ability
        and devotion to duty are in keeping with the highest traditions of the
        military service and reflect great credit upon himself, the American
        Division and the United States Army.

FOR THE COMMANDER:

OFFICIAL:

W. L. GIRVIN

T. H. TACKABERRY
Colonel, GS
Chief of Staff

# ENDURING MEMORIES

CDR Curtis Richard Dosé

My name is Curtis Richard Dose. I was a Lieutenant F-4J Phantom pilot with the United States Navy on May 10, 1972. Our Fighter Squadron VF-92 deployed on USS *Constellation* CVA-64 on Yankee Station Gulf of Tonkin Gulf for strike missions into North Vietnam. The approximate duration of our flight over Kep Airfield, NVN was five minutes. The two units involved were two VF-92 F-4Js versus two NVN Regiment 921 MiG-21s and two Soviet MiG-21. I was pilot of the VF-92 section wingman. The specific situation and that caused the criticality of the combat encounter was supersonic, then high-G extremely low-altitude dogfight over enemy airfield deep in enemy territory. The MiG-21 wingman, flown by Nguyen Van Ngai, was shot down with an AIM-9 Sidewinder and crashed with no ejection. Ngai was KIA. As a result of this particular action, I received the Silver Star.

My enduring memories are that war is hell, and we should not subject our young men to it. One hundred and ninety-one combat missions will hone fighter pilot skills to a Rambo level; if it is trying to kill you, it dies. Strong fighter pilot skills can keep you alive, but luck helps too. Fighter pilots on both sides were remarkably similar, with the same skills, fears, passion, and patriotism. I feel more aligned with the North Vietnamese pilots I fought with and later met than I do with UC Berkeley graduates.

Reflecting on my personal changes that took place over the years regarding my character, family and social relationships, perspectives, morals, and behaviors that resulted from the combat action was my relationship with my religious belief. I was an altar boy in high school and attended church at the Naval Academy. I came home from Vietnam an atheist. I could not imagine a God that would allow such carnage. A loving Catholic wife healed me back to the church twenty years later.

My father was a distinguished naval aviator and officer, who shot down a Japanese Zero in WWII and later commanded the USS *Midway*, CV-41. I believe we are the only father-son who both have aerial victories. My combat experience gave us something else to share, but we never did. He was a great dad, but he died in 1998.

I kept my feelings about Vietnam deeply inside after coming home. I didn't even know about my feelings until a TV show called something like *Welcome Home Vietnam Veterans* in the 1980s. I wanted to hear the era bands that had been invited, so I watched. It had some young actor host I knew, Robin Williams, who kicked it off with, "I was too young for Vietnam service but know you, Vietnam vets, were treated poorly coming home. We would like to welcome you home properly today." Suddenly, I was bawling like a baby as all the bad stuff came back up— watching friends and enemies die, empty ready room seats, funerals, making it home when others didn't, and delaying in the F-4 cockpit after landing and shutdown from a tough mission because my knees were shacking so badly I knew I could not safely climb down the side of the F-4, then looking up the line of parked F-4s on the carrier edge to see all the other pilots also waiting before climbing down.

In 2016, I was contacted by a pilot friend of mine that I was invited to join a group of US MiG killers planning to visit NVN

MiG pilots in Hanoi, with a chance for the US pilots to meet the NVN MiG pilots with whom they had a dogfight. I went with twelve other US pilots and met twenty NVN MiG pilots. The MiG-21 pilot I shot down was killed, and the MiG-21 flight lead had been killed a month after our engagement. The Russian MiG-21 pilots had not come forward. But I met the MiG-21 pilot who was holding his section short of the runway at Kep (whom I teased for not coming up to fight us), and a MiG-17 pilot, Tu De, who was sitting in his MiG-17 in a runway-side revetment and watched our entire dogfight with horror and amazement. He has become a good friend, and he and his wife, Hoa, have visited our home in San Diego. While in Hanoi, I was on a Vietnamese TV show that introduced me to the sister of the MiG pilot, Ngai, whom I had killed. She was very forgiving and invited me to come to their home and dine with their family. I went to their village the next day and visited Ngai's grave, leaving flowers. I then was welcomed into the family home with introductions and a many-course meal with lots of vodka toasts. After dinner, the head of the family stood up and thanked me for coming and said they were extremely proud of Ngai in 1972 as a frontline MiG-21 pilot. They were heartbroken when he had been killed, but now, forty-four years later, they had a new fighter pilot in the family, Curt Dosé, who was always welcome in their home and their hearts, heavy stuff, but with great healing and closure.

My practical advice for others who might become a combat pilot or similar team member, learn the necessary skills from your flight lead:

> *Study your enemy's capabilities and limitations but be ready for surprises.*
> *Don't blame God for man-made situations.*
> *Watch out for PTSS—don't hold "bad stuff" inside.*
> *If possible, later reconcile with your enemy.*

# BY THE GRACE
# OF GOD GO I

LT Anthony Joseph Principi, JD

My name is Anthony Joseph Principi, Lieutenant, officer-in-charge, River Patrol Unit Mekong Delta, Republic of Vietnam. My account of my war experience that served as my turning point in war and molded the nature of my character began after graduation from Annapolis in the spring of 1967. I was assigned to the USS *Joseph P. Kennedy,* Navy Gearing class destroyer (DD-850), to serve on a swift boat patrol force on the Mekong Delta. My unit was River Patrol Squadron 5. The approximate date of our mission was in August 1969. We spent a couple of days in a tent outside Tra Cu, a small Vietnamese village located on the Vam Co Dong River, the location of the US Naval Advanced Tactical Support Base west of the Cambodia border. The Angel's Wing area of Cambodia was a key stronghold in Cambodia near the Vam Co Dong River. We could not strike into Cambodia, and we had to wait until the Vietcong came across the Vam Co Dong and the Go Dau Ha Rivers to do so. My field of operations were near the Twin Rivers.

Our main mission was determined a short time later when I was ordered to emplace electric sensors along the border. These electronic-magnetic sensors, planted in strings, could register and report movements on the ground. When we got back on the swift boat, we received an emergency call from our base camp. The North

Vietnamese Army (NVA) had dug underground spider holes and trenches and had hidden in the troughs that were covered by long bamboo grass, akin to U-shaped trees that had long roots and radiated horizontally from parent plants. A US Army Special Forces team had moved into the NVA trap, and my unit was called to go into the fight. We raced to the scene of the battle, and by the time we got there, it was about over: the North Vietnam fighters had fled. I was twenty-three years old, and I had never seen such an action. I leaned up against a tree, and while I was throwing up, the tree moved. I looked down at the foot of the tree and saw a hole with two dead Vietnamese soldiers virtually staring up at me. This action was during my first forty-eight hours at base camp. There were no wounded soldiers; all were killed, so we put them in body bags. I did not know what would come next. I wondered if I would ever see my family again. We continued operations, went into action, crossed the river, and exchanged gunfire. A month later, the navy officer-in-charge at Tra Cu was killed. I was transferred to high-speed patrol boats, and we continued on doing our job.

One very bad night, we had sixteen boats at the far end of this stretch of base camp. The Vietnamese took no prisoners, and they were really tough. We were open to fire one night when we started getting incoming mortar rounds. The Vietnamese would fire on one side of the camp, then fire on the other side of the camp, and then take the center of the camp. We got ready for a ground attack. Our unit took one causality; he was my point man, Jim Kirschner, who was always in front me, and he was shot in the leg with a poisoned bullet. We got him a medic, and we ended up losing one member of my squad. By the grace of God, we did not get overrun and caught between the Army's Special Forces detachment and our team.

I will never forget seeing the images of dead men: I can still see death in their eyes and faces, still smelling their stench in the intense heat. Toward the end of my tour, we learned of a South Vietnamese encampment, and we were to turn over operations to the South Vietnamese Navy. We had been living in a virtual swamp, even having to deal with rats in our hair at night. Somehow, we had also gotten hold of a piglet, and it became a pet. The piglet got so big and so fat we sold it to the Cambodians; however, the lucky pig managed to escape the Cambodians, and it came back to our base camp!

I was awarded a Bronze Star with Combat V, awarded for valor and bravery during combat. I have been blessed and fortunate to have served under two presidents. I served as United States Secretary of Veterans Affairs. I came away with a great sense of humility. I am honored to serve our military and to help the lives of those serving today and to make tough decisions as a result of my wartime experiences. I continue to serve as the chief executive officer and president of the Principi Group, LLC.

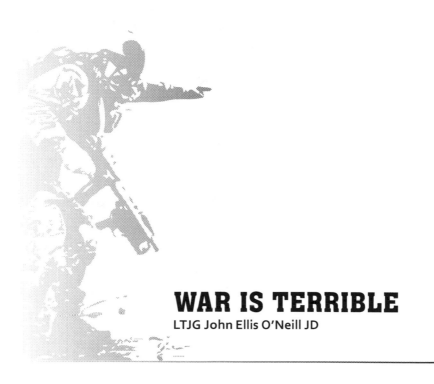

# WAR IS TERRIBLE

LTJG John Ellis O'Neill JD

My name is John Ellis O'Neill. I was a Lieutenant JG serving as an officer-in-charge of PFC 94 and later in command of the entire Swift Boat Detachment on Operation Sea Float on the Cua Dai River in the Nam Can Forest in South Vietnam. I served at that location from November 1969 until May 1970.

My unit was Coastal Division 11. Its main mission was the interdiction of North Vietnamese troops and supplies from Cambodia into the Uminhand Nam Can Forest base areas. Between March and April 1970, I was shot at and nearly killed on many occasions as a Swift Boat OIC, more than thirty-five times according to my second Bronze Star Award.

Once I awoke to find a .51 CAL bullet hole perhaps 2" above my head. On another occasion, my crew escaped annihilation by five to six 50-pound claymore mines in a small canal designed to be triggered by our passage. Likewise, in April 1970, we were targeted with more than twenty B-40 rockets, seven of which were fired. Although more than 50% of those in our unit were killed or wounded, none of these events, nor many other close calls, resulted in our deaths or serious wounds.

The incident foremost in my memory was the return of two critically wounded fellows, brown-water sailors, to our seafloat base on the Nam Cam Forest in April 1970. They were my friends. One was a chief petty officer whose shoulder was shot off by a B-40 rocket. I watched him turn gray and then die as nothing could be done to help him. A second sailor mortally wounded died mostly in my arms. I put my helmet liner under his openly wounded head as he slowly and peacefully died. I kept the bloodstained helmet liner for many years to remind me of him and his sacrifice.

The mission that resulted in their terrible wounds was a so-called psyops mission in which the boats broadcast over loudspeakers, pleas to Chu Hoi—that is to peacefully come forth. While quite humanitarian, it left the boats and sailors tremendously vulnerable by providing advanced notice to the NVA of their approach. On this occasion, it led to the disaster with numerous dead.

When I returned home in 1970–71 to teach at the NROTC unit, Holy Cross College in Massachusetts, I was confronted repeatedly by those who claimed we were baby killers. When I heard John Kerry, from our unit, claim that we were the Army of Genghis Khan, I was determined for my lost friends to set the record straight. First, in a 1970 debate with Kerry and later in 2004 as part of my fellow Swift Vets Group and author of the number 1 best seller *Unfit for Command* (that Kerry blamed with his defeat), we did set the record straight. I hope my friends, whom I believe to be in heaven, rest easier and more peacefully knowing that in their absence, we defended their honor. After 2004, after more than thirty-four years, I sent to storage the bloodstained helmet liner from that sad day on the seafloat. But I remember almost every day my good friends—the best friends of my life—whom I lost in or because of Vietnam.

What would I change? Only this. War is terrible and should be engaged in only when there is no alternative. But in a war, as McArthur stated, "there is no substitute for victory." Wars should be fought to win—not tied. If wars are not important enough to win, they should avoided.

# FIRST NIGHT IN VIETNAM

SGT Mike Rummel, JD

Was what I experienced the night of July 30–31, 1968 combat? What constitutes combat? Most certainly, what could have happened that night would have been considered combat if an exploding rocket had resulted in my being wounded or killed. So here is that story and how it affected me for the remainder of my life.

It takes many officers and enlisted personnel doing many different jobs to support a force of infantry, cannons, and tanks in combat. Combat experience is not usually associated with someone who works "in the rear" in a war zone, though combat-related actions have seeped into any and every part of a war zone in recent decades. I was asked about my experiences during the twenty-eight months I was stationed in Vietnam. Those twenty-eight months was "in the rear." For me, the most impactful happening occurred my first night in Vietnam, July 30, 1968. It involved mortars being lobbed into our sprawling Marine Corps support base known as Camp Jay K. Books at Red Beach, north of Da Nang, Vietnam. To me, that experience was at one far end of a continuum labeled "combat experience." I was asked about this experience because the requester wanted to know if, and how (assuming there was an "if"), it affected my life thereafter. It did affect my life, and I think it should be part of what any society thinks about when it mulls over the effects of war upon anyone sent to be part of it.

Nothing happens in a vacuum. The background, or context, in which an event occurs can shape our reaction to the event and help make it more, or less, meaningful in its effect upon us. With that in mind, I note that unlike the experiences of my paternal grandfather and paternal great-uncle in World War I, and my father and paternal uncle in World War II, I did not enter a war zone as part of a unit. By the time the Vietnam War affected me in July 1968, most "newbies" (me) going to Vietnam were thought of as "replacements" for someone whose tour of duty had ended. For Marines, a tour of duty in Vietnam was 13 months, or 395 days. So the 160 of us (Marines) on the Continental Boeing 707 landing at Da Nang Air Base were akin to a planeload of strangers "going off to war" in a strange land via a modern means of transportation in the time it took to fly from Kadena Air Base in Okinawa to Da Nang and not knowing anyone around us on the plane for more than a few days.

Here is where I can insert a reality that brings humor and sadness simultaneously. Today, a half century after the Vietnam War, when we board a commercial airliner, we are surrounded by a far greater hodgepodge of fellow travelers than most of us remember from the glory days of air travel. The classic in my mind was less than five years ago when I was boarding a flight from San Diego to Baltimore-Washington International Airport. A family of four—two parents, a baby, and a toddler—was boarding the flight with the baby strapped to the front of Dad, the little girl holding Mom's hand, each parent lugging a carry-on, the father pushing a collapsible stroller, and Dad with a huge cloth bag filled with stuffed toys hanging off a shoulder. One of the reasons I remember this is because my traveling companion noticed toys falling out of the sack that we recovered and handed to the clueless father. Airlines dealing with such traveling circuses fear negative public reaction if they try to limit what a family can take on board, while the rest of us haggle over the size of one carry-on bag.

The Marine Corps' way of loading a 160-passenger jet was somewhat as follows: "When I give the word, you are going to quickly, quietly, and orderly enter the plane from the access ladder. The first Marine in line will move all the way to the rear, turn to his left at the last row, proceed all the way in, sit down, shut up, and await further orders. The next Marine will sit next to him. When those three seats are filled, the next Marine will turn to his right and complete the same procedure in that side of the plane, filling each row across the body of the plane from the rear to front of the plane. There will be NO picking of seats to be near a window or on the aisle. You WILL take the next seat open as the Marine in front of you sits down in his seat. We will fill each row of empty seats on each side of the plane from the rear to the front. Do you understand me?" "YES, SIR!" was yelled in unison

I found this funny as hell when I thought of how civilians "lolly-gag" as if the world centered around each and every one of them as an individual. I took pride in the orderly Marine Corps' way of filling a plane in very few minutes. But it was also another reminder that the kind, safe world we were leaving would not be found when we deplaned for the last time in Da Nang.

Once we arrived, we were sent all over I Corps to a multitude of new posts of duty, not knowing a single person we met after having left "civilization" on the stewardess-loaded jet and going to a World War II Army cot, if lucky, or to slogging through a jungle, fighting the weather, insects, Vietcong, and one another, or to something in between. And all the petty bullshit we endure in everyday life follows us to anywhere we go in a war zone. If one is swift enough to "know" that, then his time in the Nam would be easier to understand, accept, and adjust to. If not, it was just another factor that might kill you before you "hopped that freedom bird back to the world." Whether "in the rear" or about to be ambushed in some nameless jungle, the ability and willingness to understand and accept what was increased one's likelihood of being able to adapt to that reality, and perhaps survive a war.

The flight to Vietnam began in the early evening darkness of July 29, 1968, when all of us, with seabags and orders in tow, were sent to the grass alongside the concrete runway at Kadena Air Base in Okinawa, Japan. We put our gear on the grass and were told we would go nowhere until we boarded the jet taking us to Vietnam. My recollection is we lay there on the grass until boarding the Continental jet about 0200 the morning of July 30, 1968. The context of my arrival in Vietnam began shaping up then and there. By the time we got onboard in the darkness of 0200, the rumor had completely circulated among all 160 of us. "Did you hear? The last jet that left here got hit by mortars as it was landing in Da Nang. Some guys got killed."

Whatever level of fear I was coping with at that time was ramped up with that "news." The entire trip to Vietnam was consumed with all the "what ifs" that an ignorant (of war) mind can conjure. I was doing this all on my own as I had no "buddies" around me, just other Marines I'd met a few days prior when we landed from the States to prepare for going into a war zone. Landing and taking off from Da Nang Air Base required steep descents and ascents to lessen the possibility of being hit by ground fire, coupled with maneuvering between Monkey Mountain on the west, the Hai Van Pass mountains to the north, and the open "Indian country" south of Da Nang. Now daylight as we descended, I eagerly looked at everything in sight. What I saw was a large airport with busy personnel scurrying about doing their business but NO potholes on the runway from mortar explosions and no carcass of a destroyed Boeing 707. It was business as usual at any airport. Aha, I'd been taken in by my first false rumor.

As we exited the plane at Da Nang Air Base, our flow was interrupted by an Air Force airman (three stripes) who forced his way against foot traffic, exiting the plane to enter the plane, take a seat in the very first row, and plop his orders into his lap with a look of, "I cannot leave this place fast enough." Yes. I wondered what it would be like for me in thirteen months. Meanwhile, I was deplaning to be processed for my first post of duty.

What one does in a situation like that is to mimic the behavior of the others, whether known to us or not. I was standing in line to be processed inside this huge, empty-except-for-a-counter warehouse to be sent on my way. The first experience out of the stateside-ordinary was to see a young Marine second lieutenant who appeared to be younger than me but who was wearing ragged, dusty utilities (meaning he had just come in from "the bush," so he was already a Vietnam veteran), going from one Marine to the next in line in front of me trying to convert his MPC ("military payment certificates"— paper money in denominations from a nickel, dime, quarter, dollar, five-dollar, ten-dollar, to the maximum of twenty-dollar amounts that were used in Vietnam in lieu of greenbacks in order to lessen the effect of "black market" sales) to "greenbacks," US currency that we use in everyday life in America. Even though he was an officer, no one would trade with him. He was not acting at all like the Marine officers we had seen since early on in boot camp. He was too "buddy-buddy," so he was his own worst enemy. Another lesson learned, i.e., trade greenbacks for MPC only at the authorized booths, lest one fall prey to an unknown fate involving a superior officer of unknown background, but whose very real, suspicious activity under the very noses of those charged with processing us made us raise our guard, not lower it.

I was told I would be going to Force Logistics Command (FLC) at Red Beach, nothing of which meant anything to me. It was a five- or six-mile ride on the back of a "deuce and a half," i.e., a two-and-a-half ton, stake-body truck bed, with seats lining either side, but otherwise an open-air vehicle. We went north from the air base on Route 1, the major north-south highway in South Vietnam. Ah, the sights, sounds, and smells of Vietnam. All three were the stereotypes one was shown on newsreels of the era, except the smells as one can experience them in only one manner, which is in person. The smell was a combination of garbage, urine, feces, and rotting "whatever." Getting too close to a 1950s garbage truck in America came closest to imitating the smell. And that smell permeated the landscape. Vietnamese were scurrying in all directions on mopeds, bicycles, Vespa-type scooters, the occasional small car, and of course, on foot. It was a tad overwhelming.

I was dropped at H&S Company for Force Logistics Command. I met Joe H. Lee, a clerk for H&S Company, a man currently rated 100% disabled by the Department of Veterans Affairs for PTSD-related issues having to do with incoming rockets and mortars at FLC before my arrival. Joe readily told me I was to fill his company's quota for perimeter guard duty for the month of August 1968. He had the company personnel carrier take my seabag and me to the company area. There were row upon row of hooches, with a wooden walkway over the sand dividing the rows, as walking in soft sand is tiring, very tiring. On the other end of each hooch was 4 × 4-framed sandbag bunker for protection from rocket and mortar attacks. I was told the transient hooch was at the end of a long wooden walkway.

I was wearing stateside utilities that were of the solid green version. They readily show sweat stains. I am a male who easily sweats upon exertion of any type or exposure to heat and humidity. There was a day in August 1968 when AFVN (Armed Forces Vietnam) Radio announced the temperature in Da Nang was 117 Fahrenheit. That first day in Vietnam, it was well over 100 degrees. My utility shirt was completely soaked with sweat. I stood out like a sore thumb. As I walked that very long walkway, seabag slung over one shoulder, to the transient hooch, I heard a male Hispanic voice yell out loudly in a mocking voice, "Three ninety-five," acknowledging he knew I had just arrived in Vietnam and that I had 395 days until I rotated out of the Nam back to the States. I made it to the transient hooch.

I entered it, finding a sergeant relaxing on his World War II-era army cot, the fold-up type. I took the empty cot in the middle of one side of the hooch. The sergeant welcomed me but immediately directed my attention to "our" sandbag bunker at the other end of the hooch. I walked over and looked. There was a large hole in the never-ending landscape of white sand. Our "bunker" consisted of a single layer of beach matting to cover the hole. This was the same material used to construct parts of the "border wall" separating America and Mexico in the San Diego sector during the 1994 buildup of the border wall.

There was a camouflaged poncho liner folded on my cot. That was my "blanket" for sleeping in the hooch. There would be nights in the Da Nang area in December 1968 when the temperature would drop to an overnight low in the 80s. During those nights, I would have two wool blankets and a poncho liner covering me, and my teeth would still be chattering until I built up residual heat beneath the blankets. When you spend day after day in 110+ heat, a drop to the 80s at night is a 30-degree drop that causes one to be cold. But this was my first night in Vietnam. I was so hot that I slept in the nude, with the poncho liner at my feet. My glasses, flip-flops, and undershorts were on the plywood deck beneath my rack; my utilities elsewhere out of my way. That was how it looked when I fell asleep.

Around 0200 on July 31, I was awakened to a very familiar sound. Having spent half my growing-up years in Prince George's County, Maryland, firefighting was performed by volunteer fire departments composed of everyday men who had regular day jobs. Twenty-four hours a day, seven days a week, the siren would go off with one to three rounds of the siren, each combination of one, two, or three soundings telling the volunteers who lived nearby what personnel were needed to respond to a medical emergency, fire, or combination of the two. I had heard those sounds thousands of times in my life till I left home for college at Michigan State in September 1965. There was a split-second thought of being home as the siren was exactly the sound I knew from my younger years.

The sergeant had explained the siren system to me. The COC (combat operations center) in the middle of the camp books compound had a crow's nest of sorts that was manned by a Marine, with a pair of binoculars, all night. His job was to scour the surrounding rice paddies for telltale signs of rockets or mortars being fired, which meant looking for flames at the moment of firing. When sighted, he sounded the siren. There may have been fifteen seconds before a rocket would land in the compound exploding, but those fifteen seconds could save a life.

During my month of guard duty, August 1968, I met a staff sergeant returning from a naval hospital ship off the coast of Vietnam. During July, the siren had sounded. That staff sergeant was quick to rise and head for the hooch door, seeking the shelter of his bunker. He turned to look back at his buddy, a gunnery sergeant, who was slower to rise. The staff sergeant turned in the doorway to yell, "Hurry up, gunny." As he uttered those words, a 122mm Vietcong-fired rocket exploded in the middle of that staff NCO hooch. The staff sergeant was wounded by shrapnel and would spend weeks recuperating. The gunny . . . well . . . the staff sergeant watched his entire body evaporate in the explosion. The sirens could save lives if they were heeded.

I heard the familiar siren. I jolted upward, trying to gain my wits in the matter of a second. I "knew" where I had placed my items a few hours earlier upon retiring. My next realization was the sergeant yelling to get into our hole. My next memory was being bare ass in that hole in the sand in a squatting position. Even so, the back of my head was rubbing that single layer of beach matting that was to protect us from exploding 122 (usually referred to as "One, twenty-two") mike-mikes as the hole in the sand was not that deep.

As I slowly realized where I was and what was happening, I began hearing rockets exploding in the compound. There was a momentary feeling of hope as I realized the sounds seemed to be a ways away in the compound and not near me. But I then got the full impact of what was happening. I was squatting in the nude, wearing my glasses, and holding one flip-flop in my right hand. I realized that Charlie (nickname for the "Vietcong," or "Victor Charlie") did not know me. He did not know that I was a nice guy. He did not know that I had a mother and father and sister at home who loved me. All Charlie knew was that I was the enemy, and his job was to kill me. I never felt so helpless, or so hopeless, in all my life.

After an untold number of minutes—probably ten or fifteen—the OK siren blared, a signal the sergeant informed me meant we could return to sleeping. Oh yes, I wanted nothing more than to sleep after what had just happened. My sarcasm aside, I doubt I slept any more that night.

I would have other nights when we took rockets, or Charlie "walked" mortars (a practice of firing a mortar and immediately adjusting the sights on the mortar tube to move the next impact in one direction or another to achieve more-desired results, damage-wise) through the compound. I was never wounded by such attacks. But being essentially unguided (except for mortars fired with a spotter to change the impact area), every one of us knew the next impact could be near us or on top of us. It was not over until it was over.

I came to know that if I rotated back to the States after my thirteen-month tour in Vietnam, I would be sent to Camp Lejeune, North Carolina, as the Corps tried to save on separation expenses when an enlistment ended by putting that Marine as close to his "home of record" as possible. For most Marines from the East Coast, that usually translated into Camp Lejeune near Jacksonville, North Carolina. That meant my last twenty months on active duty in the Marine Corps would be spent in North Carolina doing electronics repair work. Twenty months of doing something I hated in a state I hated being in was an unbearable thought.

Another aside relates to the PSAs (public service announcements) made on Armed Forces Vietnam Network (AFVN) to assist military personnel nearing the end of their tour of duty in Vietnam to prepare for their final days in the Nam. There was what I considered to be a humorous PSA that I loved hearing because it was given on the level of a junior enlisted man, not in formal military jargon. It involved one guy talking to his buddy about his pending rotation back to America. The beginning went something along the lines of, "Yeah, man, I've got two days and a wake-up, a bowl of cornflakes, and the ol' seabag drag, as I get on that freedom bird back to the world." I never tired of hearing that on the only AM radio station the US Military operated in Vietnam.

Vietnam turned out to be relatively safe in the Da Nang area, and there were always plenty of make-work jobs for a junior enlisted Marine in a war zone that would enable him to work outside of his MOS (military occupational specialty). I extended my tour of duty in Vietnam two times, for six months on each extension. For that I was given "thirty days free leave anywhere in the free world." That added a week before and a week after each of my two thirty-day Leaves. All totaled, my time stationed in Vietnam became almost twenty-eight months so that when I returned to the world at the end of my last extension, I had about five months of active duty remaining on my four-year enlistment. And the Marine Corps was good at giving ninety-day early outs to save more money for the government. Ultimately, I got out three months early for just that reason. But it was not until I got home from Vietnam the last time in November

1970 that that first night in Vietnam came into play in my everyday stateside life.

Throughout my high school years, my father and I, and uncles and cousins, would go deer hunting on weekends for six weeks in November and December at Camp A. P. Hill, a seventy-seven-thousand-acre US Army Reserve training base in Caroline County, Virginia. We all lived in Prince George's County, Maryland, which was the beginning of Southern Maryland. We would arise about 0200 and drive to the house of the uncle who grew up in Caroline County, Virginia. We divided up bodies and shotguns between the number of vehicles we needed and would then head out on US Route 301, going South to cross the Potomac River into Virginia where we would stop at a wayside diner for breakfast before finishing the trip to Camp A. P. Hill where we would attend their on-site training about rules, register, and then drive out to where we would set up "on stand" almost an hour before the sun appeared.

The trip, the breakfast camaraderie, the assembling with other hunters, and the drive out to go on stand combined to be just as enjoyable to me as the daylong efforts we put into deer hunting. So we had close to twenty hours of solid fun together each time we went out. We were only allowed to use shotguns at A. P. Hill. But the hunting season was six weeks long, which meant a minimum of six successive weekend trips to Camp A. P. Hill. I had missed this when I went away to college in Michigan and then when I enlisted in the Marine Corps and was no longer "home" for such activities. When I got home in late November 1970, I was looking forward to a weekend return to hunting as we had done it in the past—virtually all family.

It was all coming back to me. It had been six years since I had enjoyed all the family time doing something we all loved. I had no idea what was about to happen to me. I was out on stand-alone as we did it individually. The morning sun was shining down on an angle through the pine needles. There was sufficient movement of air so that with particles floating in the air, I could "see" the sunlight. That alone was beautiful. Then two deer came running up and halted about fifteen yards from me. I was downwind and still. They did not smell me or see me. They sniffed the air for a bit. Sensing no danger, they began grazing. The beautiful scene had become idyllic.

I slowly raised the barrel of my shotgun and put the butt of the stock into my shoulder. They were broadside to me. Aiming was easy as I brought the bead on the end of my barrel in line with the chest cavity of the larger deer. And then it hit me. Suddenly, I was in that beach-matting-protected hole in the sand at Red Beach that I had not thought that much about since it was only the first rocket attack of more to come. I remembered those feelings of helplessness and hopelessness. I could not do to another living being what I had felt in July 1968. I lowered the shotgun. I stood there and enjoyed nature at its best until they bounded off their own accord. I walked out of the woods. I never went hunting again for the remainder of my life to date. I have no desire to do so. I am now the guy who takes a paper towel and places it in the path of spiders I find in my house and then rolls up the paper towel till I get outside and can release the spider into the grass. I do not want to kill any living thing, unless forced to do so.

Perhaps that first rocket attack affected me that way because it was the first and came at the end of a several-day buildup to finally flying in—alone—into a war zone and not having anyone with whom I could process all those thoughts and feelings. Perhaps I toughened up after the first rocket attack. Regardless, those thoughts and feelings while on stand in the pine trees of Camp A. P. Hill in Virginia were unmistakable as to their long-term effect upon me.

Also, in hindsight, it took me decades to appreciate, and then acknowledge, that my reaction time is a second slower, at least, than some, most, or all other people. The significance of this is usually lost on young males who may be similarly constituted by their genes or upbringing because they, like me, were raised on those less-than-realistic (i.e., NOT *Saving Private Ryan*) war movies of the 1940s, '50s, and '60s that cast at least one male as the hero we all wanted to emulate when it came our time to shine in Vietnam. But that view of our future was unrealistic. How many men died in combat because a leader missed reacting by a second or so? Probably more than any of us want to think about. So as I aged, I was thankful to God that I had not been called upon to react in a split second, the failure of which could have cost another Marine, or sailor, his life. I am quite happy not being a hero. It is enough for me to realize that given my genetic makeup (or maybe the manner in which I was raised), I was not responsible for the loss of life of any other Marine or sailor in Vietnam.

What can I offer to others after this experience? I am uncertain. We all react in our own ways to new experiences and stress. I know that as a male growing up in the 1950s, my father and I enjoyed watching war movies on television. He had spent time in England, France, and Belgium in World War II. He would talk about noncombat, anecdotal happenings that we could laugh about and maybe relate to the movies we watched. Otherwise, I was left with my own reactions and feelings. Those movies were made to sell war bonds. They were made to keep up morale on the home front. They were meant to get guys and gals to enlist in the military as Uncle Sam needed them. And the war experiences tended to be somewhat glorified to make a good story. I had a cousin famous for not letting the truth get in the way of a good story, including those he related about his time in the US Navy. Those war movies I watched as an impressionable young boy did not let the reality of *Saving Private Ryan* come alive on the screen.

I would advise going into unknown situations with as open a mind as possible and to try not to let immediate reactions be the long-term reactions. One needs to be removed from a war zone in order to decompress, talk about what happened with others who had similar experiences, and to just let it sink in and try to recognize one's own unique reaction to a situation that is no way ever meant to be normal.

*"Semper Fidelis…!"*

# ON PATROL

CDR Warren Millard

River Squadron 55, of which I was the operations officer, was tasked with patrolling the Vinh Te Canal along the Cambodian border in Western South Vietnam. Our assignment was to thwart the effort by Vietcong (VC) and North Vietnamese Army (NVA) troops to cross the Vinh Te Canal and make their way into South Vietnam.

Our riverine patrol boats (PBRs) patrolled the canal from Chou Doc to Ha Tien on the western coast. Most of the patrols were done at night as darkness gave the enemy troops cover to cross the large areas north of the canal without being detected.

Our mission was not so much to kill the VC and NVA but rather to deter them from attempting to cross. We were mostly good white Protestant and Catholic boys, and killing people of whatever stripe was not especially appealing. We did realize, however, that killing us was fine with the VC and NVA, so that factored into our mindset as well.

One night in March 1970, we had a three-boat patrol in the canal and had taken our positions about 2100. Each boat had its bow stuck in the north bank of the canal and had two spotters on the bank with night vision watching for persons moving south across the plain toward the canal. We spotted a large group of twenty to thirty persons moving toward us. Since our mission was to deter not to kill, we began a series of star shells to light them up, alert them that we were there, and hopefully discourage their attempt to cross the canal.

The star shells followed by large-caliber weapons fire and grenades from our boat launcher did not deter them. They returned fire and continued toward our position. Our spotters on the bank jumped back in the boats, and we backed out of our position on the bank and into the canal where we had room to maneuver.

Thereafter, the PBRs made a series of high-speed runs through the area shooting up anything in sight, which was pretty much random since it was midnight dark. Each boat had twin 50-caliber machine guns, 60*mm* guns, grenade launchers, and personal weapons. There were lots of bullets flying in both directions. Hard to forget the sound of bullets flying overhead. Not sure if we killed or wounded anyone, but we suffered no casualties.

After about thirty minutes, the fire from the canal north subsided, and we stood down as well. Our assessment was that none of the VC or NVA crossed the canal that night but rather returned north. We had no South Vietnamese troops with us that night, so there was no pursuit on our part.

This particular event was not unusual. Something very close to this happened many nights while patrolling the canal. In firefights such as this, very few orders were given. Everyone knew what to do and how to do it. They knew that their survival depended on doing their job and shipmates doing their jobs.

I never really thought about the danger of being killed until months later. On scene, the focus was on training, preparing for the mission, and executing the plan. We did lose a few folks on the PBRs, and that was very sobering. While in a firefight, one was busy ducking and shooting back and making sure everything you could control was being done to protect the crew.

In the years since, I recall saying more than a few times when things weren't going as intended, "Well, it can't be too bad. No one is shooting at us!"

US military personnel spent one or two tours of one year each in Vietnam and then returned to CONUS to our nice safe lifestyles and we became concerned about relatively trivial matters. The Vietnamese people never left their homeland, and they were eventually overrun by the communists from the North Vietnam. Freedom they will never know even though thousands of Vietnamese people and we died to preserve freedom for them.

# A LIFETIME
# OF SERVICE
SP5 Charles G. Byers, BSN

My name is Charles G. Byers Jr. I served in the US Army from 1966 to 1972. After high school graduation in Houston, Texas, I enlisted in the United States Army and took my basic training at Fort Polk, Louisiana. Upon graduation, I completed by basic medical training at the Medical and Educational Training Campus (METC) located on Joint Base Fort Sam Houston, San Antonio, Texas.

As a trained combat medic, I arrived in Vietnam in July 1967 and was assigned to Charlie Co, Second Battalion, Sixtieth Infantry Regiment, Ninth Infantry Division as the senior medic. My first duty assignment in Vietnam was at a forward observation area off the Mekong River at a small base camp. I was to oversee the other medics, hold sick call, be available day and night, support operations with the infantry, and provide medical assistance to some of the civilian population.

I remember my first night in Vietnam at my duty assignment. Upon arriving almost at dusk and seeing my platform aid station and my sandbagged bunker, I was told I was the replacement medic because the Vietcong recently overran the aid station. It was night, and I had to unpack my equipment in the bunker; there were no lights, just a small flashlight illuminating my bunker. When my field phone rang, I heard a voice saying, "The cinnamon rolls are ready."

I thought this could be the code for, "We are going to be attacked." This was my first night, so I remember grabbing my steel pot, my two aid bags, and my rifle, and I waited for the war to break out. I was not sure how much time had passed, but the field phone rang again, and this time I heard, "Hey, Doc, are you coming over? I baked you some nice cinnamon rolls for you!" That was an example of the paranoia I experienced, and that was Vietnam. You were constantly looking over your shoulder everywhere and all the time.

I had twenty-three days left before I was coming home back to Texas. I was pulled out of the field and was working inside a battalion aid station and supporting the battalion surgeon when we received a message that one of our companies was hit hard and still under attack. We were immediately reassigned to serve as combat medics for the Ninth Infantry Division. They wanted the battalion surgeon and two other medics to be picked up and dropped in the rear area with extra medical supplies so we could treat all the wounded. I volunteered, and David Squires from Louisville, Kentucky, another medic, who had nine days left in Vietnam, also volunteered for this mission. Squires and I, both with Alpha Company, stepped forward to volunteer. I attempted to convince Squires he should say behind as it would be too risky, and he only had a little more than a week left of service. But Squires insisted on volunteering. To Squires, these were "his men," and he "needed to be with his men at that time."

David Squires and I were then transported by helicopter to a location near the Cambodian border. We were dropped in the wrong area, right in the middle of an ambush, with a different unit—2/39th— that had already suffered many casualties.

June 1, 1968 is a day that I will never forget. The consequences of the combat situation, and my survival that resulted in my turning point that forged my future, took place June 1, 1968. The two of us separated, and we started attending to the wounded. David Squires was a conscientious objector, meaning he did not carry a weapon and did not believe in killing. Throughout his time in Vietnam, Squires only carried a big buck knife, which he occasionally only used to strip clothes to help treat soldiers. Squires was a good medic, and he believed in healing and helping others.

I was attending to my third wounded soldier, and I had to perform a field tracheotomy, a surgical procedure that consists of making an incision on the anterior aspect of the neck and opening a direct airway through an incision in the trachea. Just as I pierced the soldier's airway, I was wounded in my left arm and stomach, and enemy fire was all around us. I suppressed the fire as best as I could. I picked up a M-79 grenade launcher and began firing at the enemy. I tried to drag out the wounded men to a small clearing; I called for medical evacuation to come in and pick up the injured. After making sure the soldier was stable, then I was able to crawl to a safe area, I gave myself morphine to ease the pain from my own injuries.

Four hours after being shot, a rescue team finally arrived, and I was able to leave the area. I was transported by helicopter to a field hospital where other medical teams were triaging injured soldiers. I remember looking up and seeing a priest giving last rites. The priest looked at me and said, "I will see you in the morning." I instantly felt relieved! This was my first hope of surviving. The next day, I was flown to Japan to receive specialized care for my wounds. It was there, in Japan, where I was told the tragic news that David Squires, at the age of twenty-two, had been killed in that ambush. David Squires had made the ultimate sacrifice for his country. This tragic loss of David affects me to this very day and remains my crucible of combat.

I am proud that I served with all my fellow brothers, and I am proud to be a Vietnam veteran, but I have never stopped serving.

My dedication to US Armed Forces veterans has continued into my civilian life, where I have dedicated my career to finding ways to help my military brothers.

After my eleven-month tour in Vietnam, I decided to remain in the medical field of the US Army. I attended the Walter Reed Army Institute of Nursing in Washington, DC. I eventually became a nurse and had the opportunity to work in the presidential ward at the prestigious Walter Reed National Military Medical Center. During the time I was there, I enjoyed meeting incredible people such as First Lady Mamie Eisenhower, wife of US president Dwight D. Eisenhower, and US senator Richard Russell. I experienced a variety of work in health care, including administrative work, but always applied my military medical experience. As a civilian, I served in the medical field for thirty-five years and eventually became a consultant.

While traveling to Washington, DC, I met Congresswoman Debbie Lesko and her district director. Congresswoman Debbie Lesko asked me if I would be willing to take on the role as her military and veterans community liaison. Although I was technically retired, I believe the position was a good way to continue my work advocating and helping my fellow veterans. My call sign in Vietnam was Big Band-Aid. I took on the role that I continue to have today, representing veterans and helping them receive the benefits they deserve for serving our country. This dedication to helping fellow veterans resulted in my honor of being inducted into the Arizona Veterans Hall of Fame, class of 2018.

In addition to being an Arizona Veterans Hall of Fame inductee, I was awarded the Silver Star, Purple Heart, and Combat Medical Badge. Aside from the veterans I aid, I still keep in contact with my fellow brothers of Alpha Company, Ninth Infantry Division. We have been through so much together, and today, all of us enjoy a special bond. We try to see one another whenever possible, and we enjoy annual reunions held in different parts of the country. We have also visited the Vietnam Memorial Wall as a group. Of course, I took that opportunity to pay homage to my fallen brother, David Squires, to whom I dedicate my story.

Charles "Doc" Byers *a.k.a.* "Big Band-Aid"
National Legislative Director, Military Order of the Purple Heart

# CLOSING

MAJ Jon M. Corey, PhD

# *Memento Vivere*

For those physically or emotionally wounded in Viet Nam, as well as in all wars—or the vast majority of citizens with no combat exposure—none of these "crucible lessons" might be of little or no consequence or value. For those of us who survived the extremes of military service in Viet Nam and in other conflicts, much has now largely faded from our collective memories, dissolved into a few sterile facts to be brought out in speeches on Memorial Day, Veterans Day, Pearl Harbor Day, Independence Day, POW/MIA Recognition Day, and Flag Day—or in a few collective book chapters of individuals' tumultuous war experiences. Our past combat actions largely go unfelt and our death gurgles go unheard and unrecalled, as they too often serve as reminders of what once was—depending on the enduring impacts seared into individuals' memories, as we now accept that "...a five-minute fire fight can last forever...!" Today, instead of sorrow and distress, and instead of seeing what human beings can do to one another in warfare, we now examine such extreme experiences with a strange blend of interest coupled with solemn reverence that are not the emotions of terrified and dying soldiers—patriots whose names are cursorily preserved in granite at The National Mall or memorialized in dozens of military cemeteries around the globe.

My having spoken extensively of individuals in actual combat, we must also recognize those vital individuals who made sure the bullets, rations, medical aid, intelligence, transportation, communications, maintenance, and every other means or resources to triumph are recognized as well. Without their services and sacrifices and their being the long, straight shaft of the arrow, no reasonable means of any victories by American armed forces, the point of the arrow, could ever be expected!

Either way, names on granite are not people, and even if they were, stone finally crumbles and slides into the sea. In the end, what soldiers, airmen, sailors, Marines, and Coast Guardsmen must share with all others is the anonymous oblivion of the "Black Hawk Down" Army RANGERS; the Minute Men at Lexington and Concord Bridge; the ranks at Gettysburg; the defenders of Troy and a myriad of combatants at known and unknown places around the world.

Being cast into the crucible creates Life turning points that are exceptional, complex, and erratic occurrences that are manifestly character-defining moments, mostly resulting in positive outcomes and transforming individuals as no other dynamics can. *In any case, they underscore the basic truths that war truly is Hell—and any other form of human endeavor is insignificant.*

Printed in the United States
by Baker & Taylor Publisher Services